God's Treasure Map: A Prayer Guide and Promises For Children
A prayer journal to empower your little one on how to pray!

Copyright © 2025 by Leticia Ababio Nortey

All rights reserved.

No part of this publication may be reproduced, stored in a retrieval system, or transmitted in any form or by any means—electronic, mechanical, photocopy, recording, or otherwise—without the prior written permission of the author, except for brief quotations used in book reviews or scholarly articles.

ISBN: 9781300598756

Published by lulu.com

This book is dedicated to guiding children on their spiritual journeys, helping them explore the beauty of prayer and God's promises.

Printed in the United States of America.

First Edition - paper back

For permissions or inquiries, please contact the author at lnortey.com

GOD'S TREASURE MAP: A PRAYER GUIDE AND PROMISES FOR CHILDREN
A PRAYER JOURNAL TO EMPOWER YOUR LITTLE ONE ON HOW TO PRAY!

Inspired and guided by the Holy Spirit of God Almighty

Written by
The mother of David, Esther, Keren, and Levi Nortey, and the wife of Michael Nortey

. . ——— ♡ ——— . .

Big thank you to all my community of support, Expanding Boundaries Team, Den of Judah Team, my parents and siblings and my paddies Anthony Domi and his wife Njeri Domi, Mrs. Yvonne Duah and family

. . ——— ♡ ——— . .

The prayers in this journal have served as a guiding resource that I have used with my children. I began teaching my son to pray as soon as he could talk and understand his words. Just as the media introduces our kids to pop culture early on, we as parents can also begin instilling in them the knowledge and teachings of their Creator, God Almighty. I truly hope your family finds joy in this book, just as I have cherished teaching my children how to pray.

Leticia Ababio Nortey ♥
lnortey.com

THIS PRAYER JOURNAL BELONGS TO

ITS A GIFT FROM

MESSAGE FROM THE GIVER:

Table of Contents

GOD'S TREASURE MAP: A PRAYER GUIDE AND PROMISES FOR CHILDREN

- The Importance of Prayer - 05
- The Curious Mind Corner - 06 - 07
- Simple Definitions for Faith-Related Words - 08
- Faith-Related Cross Word Puzzle - 09
- Gratitude for Family - 10
- Prayer Over Food and Drinks - 12
- Prayer for Next Grade, Next School Year - 14
- Prayer to Be Filled with the Heart of God - 16
- Prayer for Sunday School - 18
- Prayer for Safety at Home - 20
- Prayer for When You Wake Up from a Bad Dream - 22
- Prayer for Blessings - 24
- Prayer for When You Wake Up from a Good Dream - 26
- Prayer for When You Feel Scared - 28
- Prayer for Neighbors - 30
- Prayer Over New Clothes and Shoes - 32
- Prayer for Success in Exam or Test - 34
- Prayer for Your Friends - 36
- Prayer for Healing - 38
- Prayer to Forgive Somebody - 40
- Prayer Before Going to Bed - 42
- Prayer When I Wake Up in the Morning - 44
- Prayer for Safety at School - 46
- Prayer for Teachers - 48
- Prayer for Wisdom - 50
- Prayer Over the Word of God (Bible) -52
- Prayer for Grandparents - 54
- Prayer for your Pet - 57
- Prayer over gifts - 60
- 31 Weekly Treasure Challenges - 62
- Notes - 65
- Coloring page - 75

The Importance of Prayer, a letter from _____

Dear _____

As you grow, there are many things I want to share with you, and one of the most important is the power of prayer. Prayer is like a special conversation we have with God. It's a time when we can speak to Him, share our thoughts, ask for help, and thank Him for all the wonderful things in our lives.

Why Pray?

Prayer helps us build a relationship with God. Just like talking to your friends every day to keep your friendship strong, talking to God helps us feel close to Him. God listens to us, and through prayer, we can feel His love and guidance.
The Bible teaches us about prayer. In Matthew 6:9-13, Jesus shares The Lord's Prayer. This is a beautiful example of how we can talk to God:

> **"Our Father in heaven, hallowed be your name, your kingdom come, your will be done, on earth as it is in heaven. Give us today our daily bread. And forgive us our debts, as we also have forgiven our debtors. And lead us not into temptation, but deliver us from the evil one."**

This prayer reminds us to honor God, ask for what we need, seek forgiveness, and ask for protection.

Prayer Provides Comfort

There are moments when we might feel worried or scared. Philippians 4:6-7 says, "Do not be anxious about anything, but in every situation, by prayer and petition, with thanksgiving, present your requests to God. And the peace of God, which transcends all understanding, will guard your hearts and your minds in Christ Jesus." When you pray, you can tell God about your worries, and He will give you peace in your heart.

When to Pray?
1. Prayer can be part of every part of your day:
2. Before Meals: Thank God for the food and the people who prepared it. You can say something simple like, "Thank you, God, for this food. Bless those who have made it and help us to always be grateful."
3. In Difficult Times: If you're facing a challenge, ask God for help. You can pray, "God, please help me be brave and strong. Show me what to do."
4. In Gratitude: When something good happens, thank God for His blessings. You might say, "Thank you, God, for my family, my friends, and all the good things you provide."
5. Prayer Guides Us
6. Prayer also guides us in making good choices. By asking God for wisdom, we can decide what is right and follow a path that pleases Him. Remember, God is always there to help you, no matter what you face.

I encourage you to make prayer a part of your life. Whether you're happy, sad, or in need, remember that God is always listening and ready to help. Keep talking to Him, and you'll find that your relationship with God will grow stronger every day.

With love,

_____

THE CURIOUS MIND CORNER

Why do we plead the Blood of Jesus?
Imagine you have a big mess in your room, and you need something really strong to clean it up. The blood of Jesus is like the strongest cleaner ever, but instead of cleaning a room, it cleans our hearts and takes away sin. Jesus died on the cross for us, and His blood is so powerful that it protects us and helps us when we're scared or in trouble. The Bible says in Revelation 12:11, "They triumphed over him by the blood of the Lamb and by the word of their testimony." This means we can win against anything bad because of Jesus' blood.

When we say, "I plead the blood of Jesus," we're asking for His protection and power to help us. It's like saying, "Jesus, I trust You to take care of this!"

Why do we pray in Jesus' name?
Think about when you want something from your mom or dad, but you ask your big brother or sister to help you ask. Jesus is like that big brother who talks to God the Father for us. Jesus said in John 14:13-14, "And I will do whatever you ask in my name, so that the Father may be glorified in the Son. You may ask me for anything in my name, and I will do it."

When we pray and say, "In Jesus' name," we're asking God to hear us because Jesus made a way for us to talk to Him. It's like having a special key to open a door!

THE CURIOUS MIND CORNER

<u>Who is the Holy Spirit?</u>
The Holy Spirit is like a helper and a guide that God gives us. Imagine you're trying to do a puzzle, and someone whispers in your ear, "Try this piece here!" That's what the Holy Spirit does—He helps us make good choices and reminds us of what Jesus taught us.
Jesus said in John 14:26, "But the Helper, the Holy Spirit, whom the Father will send in my name, will teach you all things and remind you of everything I have told you."
Some people say "Holy Spirit" and others say "Holy Ghost," but they mean the same thing. The Holy Spirit is God's Spirit living in us, helping us every day.

<u>Why did Jesus talk about His body and blood with bread and wine?</u>
Before Jesus died, He had a special meal with His friends, the disciples. He gave them bread and said, "This is my body," and He gave them wine and said, "This is my blood." He wanted them to remember that He was going to die for them and for everyone in the world.
In Luke 22:19-20, Jesus said, "This is my body given for you; do this in remembrance of me... This cup is the new covenant in my blood, which is poured out for you."
When we take communion (the bread and juice at church or home), we're remembering how much Jesus loves us and that He gave His life to save us.

<u>What does all this mean for you?</u>
When you pray, you can:
- Plead the blood of Jesus to ask for protection and help.
- Pray in Jesus' name to ask God for what you need.
- Ask the Holy Spirit to guide you and help you make good choices.

And remember, Jesus loves you so much that He died for you, and His power is always with you! Amen ●

Simple Definitions for Faith-Related Words

1. Obedience – Listening to God and following what He wants us to do because we trust Him.
2. Glory – How wonderful and amazing God is! When we talk about His glory, we mean all the goodness and power that makes Him special.
3. Sacrifice – Giving up something important to show love or help someone, just like Jesus gave His life for us.
4. Redemption – When Jesus saves us from our sins and gives us a fresh start to be close to God.
5. Holy Spirit – God's invisible helper who gives us strength and teaches us how to live for Him.
6. Patience – Waiting calmly and trusting that God's timing is always right.
7. Mercy – God's kind heart for forgiving us and helping us, even when we don't deserve it.
8. Eternal – Something that lasts forever. God's love and life with Him are eternal.
9. Almighty – Another word for God that shows He is the strongest and can do anything.
10. Salvation – The special gift of being saved by Jesus so we can live forever with God.
11. Faithfulness – God always keeping His promises to us and staying with us every day.
12. Repent – Saying you're sorry to God for doing something wrong and deciding to make better choices.
13. Neighbor – Anyone around you, and God asks us to love and care for them.
14. Rejoice – Feeling so happy in your heart because of God's great love and blessings.
15. Fellowship – Spending time with other people who love God and helping each other grow in faith.
16. Covenant – A special promise between God and His people that He will always keep.
17. Scripture – Words in the Bible that God gave us to learn about Him and His plans.
18. Deliverer – A name for God or Jesus because they can save us and keep us safe.
19. Devotion – Showing God how much you love Him by giving Him your time and heart.
20. Testimony – A story someone shares about how God has helped them or changed their life.

Faith-Related Cross Word Puzzle

Almighty, Bible, Commandment, Deliverer, Devotion, Eternal, Faithfulness, Fellowship, Glory, Holy Spirit, Joy, Light, Love, Mercy, Neighbor, Obedience, Patience, Redemption, Repent, Scripture, the blood of Jesus, Jesus, Mercy

E	R	U	T	P	I	R	C	S	B	J	J	F	F
U	R	E	D	E	M	P	T	I	O	N	A	A	Y
B	W	H	B	T	T	W	G	R	H	C	I	Q	T
F	F	A	M	V	I	D	S	V	N	T	F	O	H
E	M	E	F	D	P	R	C	O	H	J	T	M	G
C	P	O	L	E	E	S	I	F	Q	N	S	P	I
N	A	V	S	L	B	T	U	P	E	N	E	N	M
E	T	A	A	I	O	L	F	P	S	K	I	M	L
I	I	M	B	V	N	W	E	J	I	Y	S	J	A
D	E	Z	E	E	Y	R	S	I	V	M	L	E	E
E	N	D	S	R	B	F	E	H	A	D	A	O	X
B	C	S	C	E	O	O	C	I	I	I	X	I	H
O	E	F	X	R	V	A	B	Z	I	P	R	G	L
Y	B	S	T	N	E	M	D	N	A	M	M	O	C

Instructions:
Find and circle each word from the list above.
Words can be hidden in any direction – up, down, left, right, diagonal, or even backward.
Enjoy discovering the words while thinking about God's love and guidance!
Have fun exploring this Word Search! Visit LNORTEY.COM for the answers

Gratitude for Family –

PSALM 107:1 – "GIVE THANKS TO THE LORD, FOR HE IS GOOD; HIS LOVE ENDURES FOREVER."

Jesus, I thank you for waking me up today.
I am grateful for life and this new day.
I thank you for my family, friends and teachers.
I blessed this day because I know you have already blessed it.
As I go out today, I pray that you watch over me
I pray you be with me everywhere I find myself
Open my heart and mind to receive and
to understand everything I learn today.
Watch over my family as I go to school
Bless my teacher and everyone in my school
Protect us from every evil
Jesus, I am yours, let your blood envelop my life today.
In Jesus Name I pray.

Today's date
SU / M / TU / W / TH / F / SA
/ /

This page allows you to share your feelings with God, including joys, worries, and dreams. God loves hearing from you, so take your time to express yourself through words, pictures, or anything meaningful to you.

God, This Is On My Heart

Prayer Over Food and Drinks

I TIMOTHY 4:4-5 – "FOR EVERY CREATURE OF GOD IS GOOD, AND NOTHING IS TO BE REFUSED IF IT IS RECEIVED WITH THANKSGIVING." (NKJV)

Dear God, thank you for my food and drink,
I thank my family for my food and drink,
I pray that you will bless this food for me
I pray that this food will nourish my body
I pray that this food will help me grow in your wisdom
I pray this food will help heal my body
and make me strong
Jesus, remove any bad thing away from the food
Jesus, thank you for giving me something to eat,
I pray that you help those who are hungry
to get something to eat too.
I plead the blood of Jesus over my food and drink in
Jesus Name I pray.

Today's date
SU / M / TU / W / TH / F / SA
_ / _ / _

This page allows you to share your feelings with God, including joys, worries, and dreams. God loves hearing from you, so take your time to express yourself through words, pictures, or anything meaningful to you.

God, This Is On My Heart

Prayer for Next Grade, Next School Year

JEREMIAH 29:11 – "FOR I KNOW THE PLANS I HAVE FOR YOU, DECLARES THE LORD, PLANS TO PROSPER YOU AND NOT TO HARM YOU, PLANS TO GIVE YOU HOPE AND A FUTURE." (NIV)

Dear God, thank You for the wonderful year of
learning and growing that has just passed.
I am so grateful for the friends, teachers, and lessons
You brought into my life. As I get ready for the next grade,
I know You have an amazing plan for me because You promised in
Your Word, "For I know the plans I have for you, plans to
prosper you and not to harm you,
plans to give you hope and a future."
Lord, I trust You with my heart and my future.
Help me to learn new things, make good choices,
and be kind to people. Blood of Jesus, protect me wherever I go
—at school, at home, and in everything I do.
Give me wisdom when I face challenges and courage
when I feel unsure. Bless my school family,
and help us work together as a team.
I pray for success in my studies and
joy in learning every lesson.
Thank You for always watching over me and
loving me. I know with You by my side,
this will be a great year!
In Jesus' name I pray. Amen.

AMEN!

Today's date

SU / M / TU / W / TH / F / SA

/ / /

This page allows you to share your feelings with God, including joys, worries, and dreams. God loves hearing from you, so take your time to express yourself through words, pictures, or anything meaningful to you.

God, This Is On My Heart

Prayer to Be Filled with the Heart of God

PROVERBS 9:10 – "THE FEAR OF THE LORD IS THE BEGINNING OF WISDOM, AND THE KNOWLEDGE OF THE HOLY ONE IS UNDERSTANDING." (NKJV)

Dear God,
Thank You for being so loving and kind to us.
You are holy, wise, and perfect in all Your ways.
Help me to always have a heart that honors and respects You.
I want to grow in wisdom, just as You said in Your Word, "The fear of the Lord is the beginning of wisdom, and the knowledge of the Holy One is understanding." Please teach me to know You better and understand how wonderful You are. Help me to always make choices that bring You joy. Show me how to listen to Your voice and follow Your ways, even when it's hard.
Lord, fill me with a deep love and respect for You so that I can grow in wisdom and understanding. Help me to remember that You are always with me and that Your plans for me are good.
Thank You for being my guide and my protector.
I love You, Lord, and I ask this in Jesus' name.
Amen.

AMEN!

Today's date

SU / M / TU / W / TH / F / SA

__ / __ / __

This page allows you to share your feelings with God, including joys, worries, and dreams. God loves hearing from you, so take your time to express yourself through words, pictures, or anything meaningful to you.

God, This Is On My Heart

Prayer for Sunday School

PSALM 119:105 – "YOUR WORD IS A LAMP TO MY FEET AND A LIGHT TO MY PATH." (NKJV)

Dear God,
Thank You for giving us Your Word,
the Bible, to guide us.
Just like a lamp lights up the dark,
Your Word helps us see the right way to go.
Please help us to understand
and follow what You teach us.
Let Your light shine in our hearts so we can
share Your love with others. Bless our
Sunday School teachers and friends
as we learn more about You today.
In Jesus' Name, Amen.

Today's date

SU / M / TU / W / TH / F / SA

___ / ___ / ___

This page allows you to share your feelings with God, including joys, worries, and dreams. God loves hearing from you, so take your time to express yourself through words, pictures, or anything meaningful to you.

God, This Is On My Heart

Prayer for Safety at Home

PSALM 91:9-10 – "BECAUSE YOU HAVE MADE THE LORD, WHO IS MY REFUGE, EVEN THE MOST HIGH, YOUR DWELLING PLACE, NO EVIL SHALL BEFALL YOU." (NKJV)

Dear God,
Thank You for being our refuge and safe place.
We trust You to watch over our home and keep us safe.
Please protect our family from anything that might harm us.
Help us feel Your love and peace all around us.
I plead the blood of Jesus over our home.
God be a mighty shield around us.
Thank You for always being with us,
no matter where we are.
We love You and are so glad that You are our protector.
In Jesus' Name, Amen.

Today's date
SU / M / TU / W / TH / F / SA

___ / ___ / ___

This page allows you to share your feelings with God, including joys, worries, and dreams. God loves hearing from you, so take your time to express yourself through words, pictures, or anything meaningful to you.

God, This Is On My Heart

Prayer for When You Wake Up from a Bad Dream

PSALM 91:11 – "FOR HE WILL COMMAND HIS ANGELS CONCERNING YOU TO GUARD YOU IN ALL YOUR WAYS."

Dear Jesus, Thank you for being with me tonight.
I had a bad dream, and I woke up feeling scared.
Please help me to feel your peace and comfort.
I know that you love me and are always watching over me.
Just as Psalm 91:11 says, "For he will command his angels concerning you to guard you in all your ways."
I believe your angels are with me, keeping me safe.
Please remove my fear and fill my heart with your love and peace.
Help me remember that you are always near,
protecting and strengthening me.
I plead the blood of Jesus over my dreams,
and I pray to cancel and reject every bad dream I had.
Thank you for your never-ending love and care.
In Jesus' name, I pray, Amen.

Today's date

SU / M / TU / W / TH / F / SA

/ / /

This page allows you to share your feelings with God, including joys, worries, and dreams. God loves hearing from you, so take your time to express yourself through words, pictures, or anything meaningful to you.

God, This Is On My Heart

Prayer for Blessings

NUMBERS 6:24-26 - "THE LORD BLESS YOU AND KEEP YOU; THE LORD MAKE HIS FACE SHINE UPON YOU, AND BE GRACIOUS TO YOU." (NKJV)

Dear God,
Thank you for your love and for the many ways you bless us every day. I am so grateful for your kindness and for always taking care of me. Today, I pray that you bless me, my family, and my friends.

Please keep us safe in your arms and let us feel your love in our hearts. Shine your light on us and guide us in everything we do. Be kind and gracious to us, and help us to share your blessings with others.

Thank you for always being with me and for filling my life with good things. I trust you, Lord, and I am so blessed to call you my God.

Amen.

Today's date

SU / M / TU / W / TH / F / SA

_/_/_

This page allows you to share your feelings with God, including joys, worries, and dreams. God loves hearing from you, so take your time to express yourself through words, pictures, or anything meaningful to you.

God, This Is On My Heart

Prayer for When You Wake Up from a Good Dream

PSALM 126:2 - "OUR MOUTHS WERE FILLED WITH LAUGHTER, OUR TONGUES WITH SONGS OF JOY,"

Dear God,
Thank you for the beautiful dream I had last night.
I woke up feeling joyful and grateful for the happiness you brought into my heart.
Just as Psalm 126:2 says, "Our mouths were filled with laughter, our tongues with songs of joy,"
I am filled with joy and laughter
because of the dream you gave me.
Please help me carry this happiness throughout my day and spread your love and joy to everyone around me.
I am so thankful for your blessings and the dreams that remind me of your goodness. I pray in Jesus name that your will and purpose for my life, and loved ones be made perfect and fulfilled
In Jesus' name, I pray, Amen.

Today's date

SU / M / TU / W / TH / F / SA

/ / /

This page allows you to share your feelings with God, including joys, worries, and dreams. God loves hearing from you, so take your time to express yourself through words, pictures, or anything meaningful to you.

God, This Is On My Heart

Prayer for When You Feel Scared

ISAIAH 41:10 – "FEAR NOT, FOR I AM WITH YOU; BE NOT DISMAYED, FOR I AM YOUR GOD."

Dear Heavenly Father,
thank you for always being with me.
I feel scared and alone, but I know that you are right
here beside me. Isaiah 41:10 reminds me, "Fear not, for I
am with you; Be not dismayed, for I am your God."
I find comfort in knowing that you are my God
and you are always here to protect me.
Please take away my fears and fill my heart
with your peace and strength.
Help me to remember that I am never alone,
and you are always watching over me.
JESUS, I AM YOURS!
Thank you for keeping me safe and for your endless love.
In Jesus' name, I pray, Amen.

Today's date
SU / M / TU / W / TH / F / SA
__ / __ / __

This page allows you to share your feelings with God, including joys, worries, and dreams. God loves hearing from you, so take your time to express yourself through words, pictures, or anything meaningful to you.

God, This Is On My Heart

Prayer for Neighbors

MARK 12:31 – "LOVE YOUR NEIGHBOR AS YOURSELF. THERE IS NO COMMANDMENT GREATER THAN THESE." (NIV)

Dear Heavenly Father, I thank You for the wonderful neighbors You have placed around me. I am grateful for their kindness, their smiles, and the ways they make our community feel like home. Thank you for keeping me safe and for your endless love. Lord, I pray that You bless each of them abundantly. Bless their homes with peace, their families with love, and their lives with joy. Protect them from harm and surround them with Your mighty angels.
In Jesus' name, I pray, Amen.

Today's date
SU / M / TU / W / TH / F / SA
__ / __ / __

This page allows you to share your feelings with God, including joys, worries, and dreams. God loves hearing from you, so take your time to express yourself through words, pictures, or anything meaningful to you.

God, This Is On My Heart

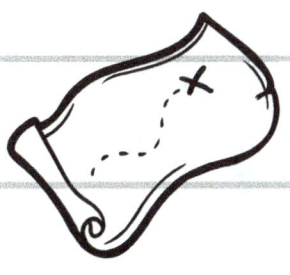

Prayer Over New Clothes and Shoes

MATTHEW 6:31-32 - "DO NOT WORRY, SAYING, 'WHAT WILL WE WEAR?' YOUR FATHER IN HEAVEN KNOWS WHAT YOU NEED."

Dear God, thank You so much for my new clothes and shoes! I am happy and excited to wear them, and I am grateful to have them.
Lord, I ask You to bless them and help me take care of them. I plead the blood of Jesus over them, I pray that you cleanse them for me.
Thank You for always knowing what I need and taking care of me.
I also pray for other children who might need clothes or shoes. Please take care of them and give them what they need too. Thank You for always being a loving Father to everyone.
I'm so thankful, Jesus. I love You, and I trust that You will always care for me.
Amen.

joy

Today's date

SU / M / TU / W / TH / F / SA

___ / ___ / ___

This page allows you to share your feelings with God, including joys, worries, and dreams. God loves hearing from you, so take your time to express yourself through words, pictures, or anything meaningful to you.

God, This Is On My Heart

Prayer for Success in Exam or Test

PHILIPPIANS 4:13 – "I CAN DO ALL THIS THROUGH HIM WHO GIVES ME STRENGTH." (NIV)

Dear God, thank you for being with me as
I prepare for my exams.
I know that with your help, I can do my best.
Philippians 4:13 reminds me, "I can do all this through him who gives me strength." Holy Spirit give me the strength and focus I need to study well. Help me to remember everything I have learned.
Help me to stay calm and confident during my exams, knowing that you are by my side. I trust that you will guide me and help me use my knowledge wisely.
Thank you for your love and support, and for giving me the courage to succeed.
In Jesus' name, I pray, Amen.

Today's date

SU / M / TU / W / TH / F / SA

___ / ___ / ___

This page allows you to share your feelings with God, including joys, worries, and dreams. God loves hearing from you, so take your time to express yourself through words, pictures, or anything meaningful to you.

God, This Is On My Heart

Prayer for Your Friends

PROVERBS 17:17 – "A FRIEND LOVES AT ALL TIMES, AND A BROTHER IS BORN FOR A TIME OF ADVERSITY."

Dear Lord, thank you for the wonderful friends you have
blessed me with. I am grateful for their love and
support in my life.
Proverbs 17:17 reminds me, "A friend loves at all times,
and a brother is born for a time of adversity."
I am thankful for friends who play and learn with me.
Please help me to be a loving and
supportive friend in return.
Jesus, guide us to grow together
in kindness and understanding.
Let our friendships be a reflection of your
love and grace. Holy Ghost Fire envelope around us.
Bless my friends with happiness and strength,
and help us to always uplift each other.
In Jesus' name, I pray, Amen.

Today's date

SU / M / TU / W / TH / F / SA

___/___/___

This page allows you to share your feelings with God, including joys, worries, and dreams. God loves hearing from you, so take your time to express yourself through words, pictures, or anything meaningful to you.

God, This Is On My Heart

Prayer for Healing

JEREMIAH 17:14 – "HEAL ME, O LORD, AND I SHALL BE HEALED; SAVE ME, AND I SHALL BE SAVED, FOR YOU ARE MY PRAISE." (NKJV)

Dear Lord Jesus, I feel very weak today, and I pray for your touch.
I need healing for (list where you are feeling pain):

.

God, my body, my soul and spirit are all made by you, I pray you bring comfort and peace back into my life. I pray you take away every pain in Jesus Name. I plead the blood of Jesus over my body. I pray over every medicine I take, that God you will back it up with your healing anointing. Jesus, I am yours, please help me to feel better. Help my doctor and the adults in my life to understand how they can help me to feel better. God I pray you take away every germ and disease from my body in Jesus Name I pray.

Today's date
SU / M / TU / W / TH / F / SA
__/__/__

This page allows you to share your feelings with God, including joys, worries, and dreams. God loves hearing from you, so take your time to express yourself through words, pictures, or anything meaningful to you.

God, This Is On My Heart

Prayer to Forgive Somebody

EPHESIANS 4:32 - "AND BE KIND TO ONE ANOTHER, TENDERHEARTED, FORGIVING ONE ANOTHER, EVEN AS GOD IN CHRIST FORGAVE YOU." (NKJV)

Dear God, today I felt hurt by something someone did Write who hurt you and what they did to hurt you:.

God, I don't know if they intentionally did that to hurt me, but their actions makes me feel (circle how you feel):

Angry/ Sad/ confused/ Hurt / Betrayed / Neglected/ Ashamed

I am finding it very hard to forgive, because I still feel hurt by their actions. I pray you help them treat me and everyone around them nicely. I pray you heal my heart from the hurt I am feeling, and help me to forgive them. Jesus please fill my heart with gladness and take away the pain.

Today's date

SU / M / TU / W / TH / F / SA

/ /

This page allows you to share your feelings with God, including joys, worries, and dreams. God loves hearing from you, so take your time to express yourself through words, pictures, or anything meaningful to you.

God, This Is On My Heart

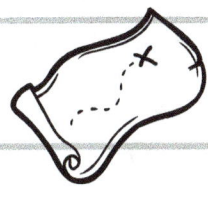

Prayer Before Going to Bed

PSALM 91:1-2 - "HE WHO DWELLS IN THE SECRET PLACE OF THE MOST HIGH SHALL ABIDE UNDER THE SHADOW OF THE ALMIGHTY." (NKJV)

Dear God, thank you for taking care of me and my family throughout the day.
It's time for me to go to bed, and
I need you to watch over me.
I pray you watch over our home and my family. I pray your mighty hands cover us as we sleep. I pray and plead the blood of Jesus over my bed and pillow. The blood of Jesus covers me, the Blood of Jesus fights for me, and the Blood of Jesus protects me. I pray against bad dreams. Jesus, I pray for sweet dreams. I pray you help me wake up on time and prepare for the new day. God, my family and I dwell in your secret place for safety in Jesus Name

Today's date
SU / M / TU / W / TH / F / SA
__ / __ / __

This page allows you to share your feelings with God, including joys, worries, and dreams. God loves hearing from you, so take your time to express yourself through words, pictures, or anything meaningful to you.

God, This Is On My Heart

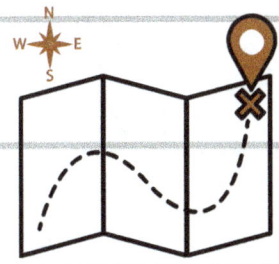

Prayer When I Wake Up in the Morning

PSALM 5:3 – "MY VOICE YOU SHALL HEAR IN THE MORNING, O LORD; IN THE MORNING I WILL DIRECT IT TO YOU, AND I WILL LOOK UP." (NKJV)

Good morning Jesus, good morning Lord, good morning angels of God. It feels great to wake up. Thank you God for waking me up. I am so thankful to be alive today and to feel your love in my heart. Please watch over me today as I go about my day. Keep me safe and protect my family and friends too. Help me to listen, learn, and do my best. Open my heart to be kind and to share your love with others. Jesus, walk with me and guide me. Make me strong and brave to face whatever comes my way. I love you, Jesus, and I trust you with my whole day. Amen.

Today's date
SU / M / TU / W / TH / F / SA
__ / __ / __

This page allows you to share your feelings with God, including joys, worries, and dreams. God loves hearing from you, so take your time to express yourself through words, pictures, or anything meaningful to you.

God, This Is On My Heart

Prayer for Safety at School

PROVERBS 18:10 – "THE NAME OF THE LORD IS A STRONG TOWER; THE RIGHTEOUS RUN TO IT AND ARE SAFE." (NKJV)

Dear God, as I go to school today, I place my school into your hands. I pray that you watch over my school and protect it from bad people. Jesus, I pray to help the grown-ups secure our school. I pray that you fill our school with your peace and love. Please give my teachers wisdom to guide us and help them teach us well. Bless my friends and classmates. Please help us to be kind to one another, to share, and to make school a happy place. Keep everyone safe and strong, and surround our school with your angels in Jesus Name I pray.

AMEN!

Today's date
SU / M / TU / W / TH / F / SA
__ / __ / __

This page allows you to share your feelings with God, including joys, worries, and dreams. God loves hearing from you, so take your time to express yourself through words, pictures, or anything meaningful to you.

God, This Is On My Heart

Prayer for Teachers

PROVERBS 2:6 – "FOR THE LORD GIVES WISDOM; FROM HIS MOUTH COME KNOWLEDGE AND UNDERSTANDING." (NIV)

Dear God, today I want to bring all my teachers and everyone who is helping me to grow and learn before you.
Thank you for placing me in their care to help me understand our world.
I know I am young and will need them to grow and learn from them. I pray that you continue to watch over them and give them the wisdom they can teach us. I pray that you bless them with more blessings and help them to be great teachers for us, the little ones.
In Jesus' Name, I pray.

AMEN!

Today's date

SU / M / TU / W / TH / F / SA

___ / ___ / ___

This page allows you to share your feelings with God, including joys, worries, and dreams. God loves hearing from you, so take your time to express yourself through words, pictures, or anything meaningful to you.

God, This Is On My Heart

Prayer for Wisdom

JAMES 1:5 - "IF ANY OF YOU LACKS WISDOM, LET HIM ASK OF GOD, WHO GIVES TO ALL LIBERALLY AND WITHOUT REPROACH, AND IT WILL BE GIVEN TO HIM." (NKJV)

Dear God,
I trust in Your promise to give wisdom when I ask. Please help me make good choices and fill my heart and mind with Your understanding, especially in tough times.
Teach me to listen to Your guidance and to act with kindness, bravery, and love.
Thank You for Your generosity in providing wisdom.
I love You, Lord, and ask this in Jesus' name.
Amen.

Today's date
SU / M / TU / W / TH / F / SA
__/__/__

This page allows you to share your feelings with God, including joys, worries, and dreams. God loves hearing from you, so take your time to express yourself through words, pictures, or anything meaningful to you.

God, This Is On My Heart

Prayer Over the Word of God (Bible)

2 TIMOTHY 3:16 – "ALL SCRIPTURE IS GIVEN BY INSPIRATION OF GOD, AND IS PROFITABLE FOR DOCTRINE, FOR REPROOF, FOR CORRECTION, FOR INSTRUCTION IN RIGHTEOUSNESS." (NKJV)

Dear Lord,
Thank you for the Bible, Your Word that directs us in living a righteous life. I ask that you grant me the strength to engage with Your Word.
I cover Your Word in the blood of Jesus.
God, please help me to comprehend what I read.
I pray that as I immerse myself in Your Word, my body, soul, and spirit will unite with it.
Jesus, guide me as I read and instill in me the joy of exploring Your Word. In Jesus' Name, I pray.

Today's date
SU / M / TU / W / TH / F / SA
__ / __ / __

This page allows you to share your feelings with God, including joys, worries, and dreams. God loves hearing from you, so take your time to express yourself through words, pictures, or anything meaningful to you.

God, This Is On My Heart

Prayer for Grandparents

PROVERBS 17:6 – "CHILDREN'S CHILDREN ARE A CROWN TO THE AGED, AND PARENTS ARE THE PRIDE OF THEIR CHILDREN." (NIV)

Dear God, today I want to pray for my grand parents. List names of Grand parents:.

I pray that you bless them, and continue to watch over them. Jesus, I pray that you shower your blessing on them. Jesus I pray to protect them from every evil. Jesus, thank you for my grand parent, and Jesus please bless them for me, I love my grand parents so much.
Jesus Name I pray

Draw a picture of you with any of your grand parent or all of them, and write why you love them.

Today's date

SU / M / TU / W / TH / F / SA

___ / ___ / ___

This page allows you to share your feelings with God, including joys, worries, and dreams. God loves hearing from you, so take your time to express yourself through words, pictures, or anything meaningful to you.

God, This Is On My Heart

Prayer for your Pet

PROVERBS 12:10 – "THE RIGHTEOUS CARE FOR THE NEEDS OF THEIR ANIMALS, BUT THE KINDEST ACTS OF THE WICKED ARE CRUEL" (NIV)

Dear Lord Jesus, I pray for my companion

Write the name or names of all the pet in your home or life.

- ------------------------------
- ------------------------------
- ------------------------------
- ------------------------------

Blood of Jesus envelope around our pet(s). Jesus, keep our pet safe from injury and every harmful situation. God, I pray that you help all of us to be there for our little friends. Help us to show your love to our little friends. I pray for healing and blessing for our pet. Jesus Name I pray

Draw a picture of you with any of your pet or pets, and write why you love them.

Today's date
SU / M / TU / W / TH / F / SA
__ / __ / __

This page allows you to share your feelings with God, including joys, worries, and dreams. God loves hearing from you, so take your time to express yourself through words, pictures, or anything meaningful to you.

God, This Is On My Heart

Prayer over gifts

JAMES 1:17 – "EVERY GOOD GIFT AND EVERY PERFECT GIFT IS FROM ABOVE, AND COMES DOWN FROM THE FATHER OF LIGHTS." (NKJV)

Dear God, I thank you for the following gifts

1. _____
2. _____
3. _____
4. _____

I pray that you bless the giver, I am truly grateful
I pray and plead the blood of Jesus of the gifts
I pray and bless them, that they will be a blessing to me and anyone who uses them. Jesus, I am grateful, help me to use them wisely
Help me to keep them safe without destroying them.
Jesus Name I pray

Today's date

SU / M / TU / W / TH / F / SA

__ / __ / __

This page allows you to share your feelings with God, including joys, worries, and dreams. God loves hearing from you, so take your time to express yourself through words, pictures, or anything meaningful to you.

God, This Is On My Heart

31 WEEKLY TREASURE CHALLENGES

How to Use the 31 Weekly Treasure Challenges

Hey there, treasure hunter! Each week, your mission is to pick one of these fun challenges and complete it with excitement and joy. These activities are like little treasures that help your heart grow closer to God.

Here's what to do:
1. Start your week by choosing one challenge—read it carefully and think about how you'll do it.
2. Take your time during the week to complete the challenge. Be creative and have fun while you do it!
3. At the end of the week, think about what you learned from the challenge. Did it help you feel God's love? Was there something special that happened?

Remember, these challenges are all about discovering how much God loves you and how you can share that love with others. Get ready to grow, shine, and smile with each week's treasure! You're going to do an amazing job!

31 WEEKLY TREASURE CHALLENGES

- [ ] Pray for Someone New – Pick a different person each day this week and say a special prayer for them.
- [ ] Nature Hunt – Discover 3 things in nature that show how amazing God is, and draw them in your notebook.
- [ ] Kindness Mission – Find one new way each day to show kindness, like helping someone or saying something uplifting.
- [ ] Verse Memory Adventure – Memorize a short Bible verse and teach it to someone in your family.
- [ ] Thankfulness List – Write or draw 5 things you're thankful for this week and share them during family time.
- [ ] Joy Jar – Fill a jar with notes of happy moments from the week to remind you of God's blessings.
- [ ] Prayer Drawing – Draw a picture for each prayer request you have, like a friend, family, or pet.
- [ ] Hidden Blessings Detective – Look for small ways God has blessed you – like a sunny day or a kind word from a friend!
- [ ] Share God's Love – Create a card or drawing that shows God's love and give it to someone.
- [ ] Quiet Time with God – Spend 5 minutes each day in a quiet place talking to God about your week.
- [ ] Helping Hands Challenge – Volunteer to help a sibling, parent, or neighbor with something they need.
- [ ] Mountain of Gratitude – Every day, write one thing you're thankful for, and by the end of the week, pile them up like a mountain!
- [ ] Nature Inspiration Drawing – Find something in nature that reminds you of God and create an art piece about it.
- [ ] Kind Words Challenge – Make it your goal to say only kind and loving words this week, even if it's hard!
- [ ] God's Love Treasure Hunt – Hide messages around your home with Bible verses about love, and encourage your family to find them.
- [ ] Worship Moves – Dance or create movements to your favorite worship song to celebrate God with your energy!
- [ ] Bible Story Roleplay – Act out a Bible story with friends or family and talk about what you learned from it.

- ☐ Secret Prayer Partner – Choose someone to pray for in secret this week. Don't tell them, just pray!
- ☐ Create Your Own Psalm – Write or draw your own praise to God, telling Him why you love Him.
- ☐ Wise Choices Jar – For each good decision you make, write it down and add it to your jar. By the week's end, count them all!
- ☐ God's Creations Collage – Draw pictures or cut out images of God's creations to make a colorful collage.
- ☐ Acts of Giving – Share something you love, like a toy or snack, with a friend or sibling this week.
- ☐ Light of the World Challenge – Every time you brighten someone's day, like through a smile or a kind word, mark it on a star-shaped card.
- ☐ Memorize & Share Scripture – Choose a Bible verse to memorize and tell a family member what it means to you.
- ☐ Habit of Gratitude Game – Before bed, see who in your family can name the most things they're thankful for that day!
- ☐ God's Promises Adventure – Pick a promise from the Bible and reflect on how you've seen it in your life this week.
- ☐ Blessings Bracelet – Make a simple bracelet with beads or string, and every time you look at it, say a prayer of thanks.
- ☐ Prayer Walk – Take a walk with a parent or friend and pray as you go, thanking God for what you see.
- ☐ Holy Helper Competition – Compete with family members to see who can be the most helpful around the house this week!
- ☐ Heart of Forgiveness – Think of something or someone you need to forgive, talk to God about it, and release it to Him.
- ☐ Shine Bright Challenge – End the month by writing or drawing about one way you shine for God and make others smile!

NOTES

DATE: _____

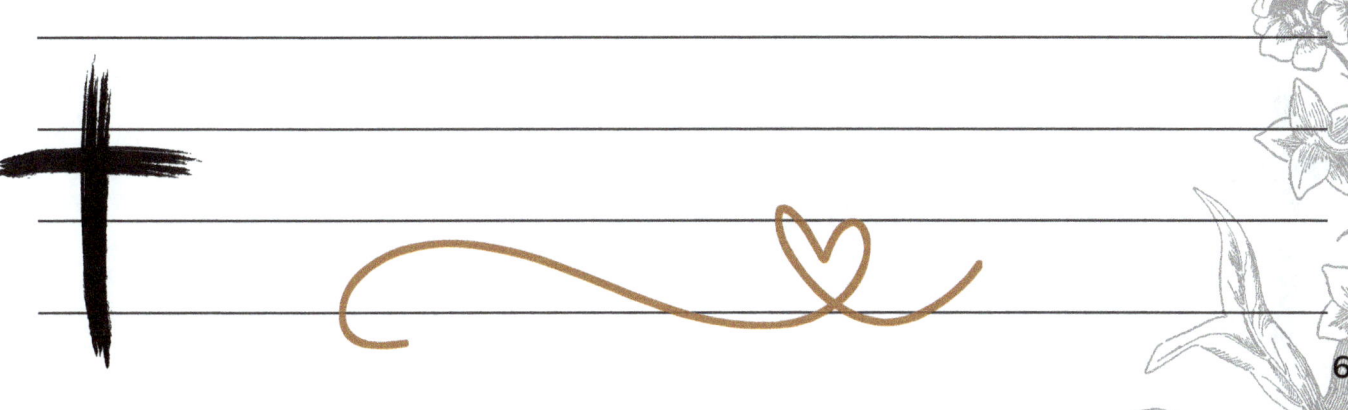

NOTES

DATE:

NOTES

DATE:

NOTES

DATE:

NOTES

DATE:

NOTES

DATE:

NOTES

DATE:

NOTES

DATE:

NOTES

DATE:

NOTES

DATE:

NOTES

DATE:

NOTES

DATE:

www.ingramcontent.com/pod-product-compliance
Lightning Source LLC
LaVergne TN
LVHW061343060426
835512LV00016B/2645